Pocket Books

In█████s

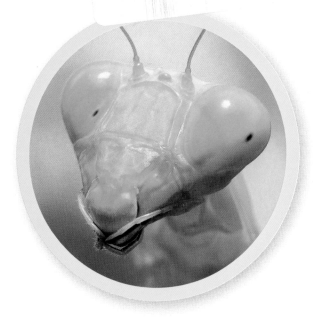

Kane Miller
A DIVISION OF EDC PUBLISHING

First American Edition 2015
Kane Miller, A Division of EDC Publishing

Copyright © Green Android Ltd 2014

For information contact:
Kane Miller, A Division of EDC Publishing
P.O. Box 470663
Tulsa, OK 74147-0663
www.kanemiller.com
www.edcpub.com
www.usbornebooksandmore.com

Printed and bound in China, January 2016
3 4 5 6 7 8 9 10
Library of Congress Control Number: 2014950299
ISBN: 978-1-61067-386-0

Images © Fotolia.com: colorado potato beetle © ALCOM; hummingbird hawkmoth © Alexandr; conehead mantis © bisantiko; small copper butterfly © chris2766; honey bee © Christian Pedant; black garden ant © claffra; emerald damselfly © Colette; hercules beetle © Cosmin Manci; garden tiger moth © creativenaturemedia; common brimstone © Die Fotografin; flightless dung beetle © Duncan Noakes; common field grasshopper © emjay smith; common mayfly © fabiosa_93; broad-bodied chaser © FLORIAN ANDRONACHE; tiger swallowtail © ganko; cinnabar moth © Gert Vrey; stag beetle © Graham Taylor; great diving beetle © Gucio_55; harlequin Ladybug © hakoar; common silverfish, common earwig © Henrik Larsson; green shield bug © JGade; common crane fly © john barber; devil's coach horse beetle © jscalev; fiddler beetle © jsm; japanese beetle © Judy Whitton; blue-winged grasshopper, tanbark borer © M.R. Swadzba; cereal leaf beetle © McCarthys_PhotoWorks; green tiger beetle © Michael Pettigrew; seven-spot Ladybug © Michael Tieck; pond skater © mite; buff-tailed bumble bee © modul_a; common clubtailed © panvart; common hawker © Parato; praying mantis © Pavlo Vakhrushev; june beetle © Piotr Kozikowski; green lacewing © pitris; apollo butterfly © psamtik; aphid © radub85; emperor dragonfly, large red damselfly © Roque141; monarch butterfly © Steve Byland; twenty-two spot Ladybug © stoupa; mole cricket © ulkan.

Images © shutterstock.com: emerald ash borer © A.S.Floro; giant cockroach, hissing cockroach © Aleksey Stemmer; scarce swallowtail © AlessandroZocc; meadow grasshopper © Andre Mueller; red wood ant © Andrey Pavlov; blue-spotted tiger beetle © asyrafazizan; giant wood wasp © Bahadir Yeniceri; mydas fly © Barry Blackburn; luna moth © Cathy Keifer; common glow worm © Cesar_Torres; cicada © Christian Musat; housefly © claffra; red admiral © Claudia Steininger; forest caterpillar hunter © Cosmin Manci; giant ichneumon © CreativeNature.nl; european hornet © Cristian Gusa; blue ground beetle © Daniel Prudek; green darner © David Byron Keener; migratory locust © David Dohnal; banded demoiselle © David J Martin; common house mosquito © Dmitrijs Bindemanis; green cone-headed planthopper © Doug Lemke; harlequin bug, oriental cockroach, eastern amberwing, cicada killer wasp © Elliotte Rusty Harold; european wasp © emer; beautiful demoiselle © ethylalkohol; black oil beetle © Florian Andronache; timberman beetle, dor beetle © Gucio_55; burying beetle, cream-spot Ladybug, poplar leaf beetle, clover springtail, fine streaked bugkin, death watch beetle © Henrik Larsson; violet ground beetle © InavanHateren; northern walkingstick © IrinaK; common green capsid © JGade; giant peacock moth © Kharkhan Oleg; great green bush cricket © koi88; asian long-horn beetle; common backswimmer © Marek R. Swadzba; peppered moth, adonis blue © Martin Fowler; slender skimmer © Mathisa; predatory bush cricket © Matteo photos; leaf-cutter ant © Micha Klootwijk; eastern hercules beetle © Ming-Hsiang Chuang; giant burrowing cockroach, death's head cockroach © Mirek Kijewski; siamese rhinoceros beetle © Mr. SUTTIPON YAKHAM; painted lady butterfly © Olha Insight; giant mesquite bug © Pearson Art Photo; large pine weevil © PeterVrabel; valley carpenter bee © photodoctor; water scorpion © QiuJu Song; bald-faced hornet © Randimal; flame skimmer © Richard A McMillin; dogbane leaf beetle, large milkweed bug © Ron Rowan Photography; green carab beetle © Sandra Caldwell; true katydid © Sari ONeal; common wasp © siloto; common water strider © skynetphoto; paper wasp, bluebottle © Sonja M; periodical cicada © Steve Byland; tawny earwig © Tomatito; caterpillar hunter © Tyler Fox. giraffe weevil © Axel Strauß / Wikimedia Commons / CC-BY-SA-3.0 / GFDL

Introducing insects

While insects are relatively small in size compared to many animal groups, they can be considered the most successful animals, as they live in almost every habitat on Earth. Most insects live on land or in the air, but there are some that live in water too. Most insects hatch from eggs. After hatching they go through different stages of development before they become adults.

Dung beetles recycle nutrients into the soil by burying animals' dung.

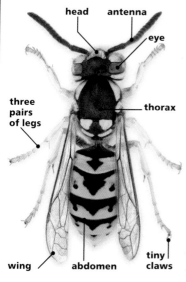

head · antenna · eye · thorax · three pairs of legs · wing · abdomen · tiny claws

Like all insects, the European wasp has three main body parts.

Characteristics of insects

Typical adult insects have 3 pairs of legs and usually 2 sets of wings. Their bodies are divided into 3 segments, each with a different function.

The head contains the brain and the eyes. The two antennae are attached to the head.

The thorax is the main body section. This section operates the wings and legs. The legs attach to the thorax.

The abdomen is the segmented tail area of an insect. It contains the insect's digestive system and reproductive organs.

3

How to use this book

The pages of this book include concise information and key features on insects from around the world.

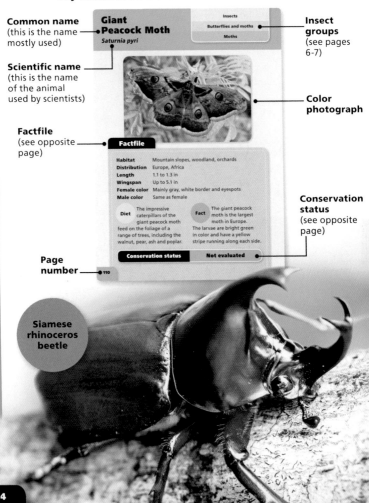

Common name
(this is the name mostly used)

Giant Peacock Moth
Saturnia pyri

Insects
Butterflies and moths
Moths

Insect groups
(see pages 6-7)

Scientific name
(this is the name of the animal used by scientists)

Color photograph

Factfile
(see opposite page)

Factfile

Habitat	Mountain slopes, woodland, orchards
Distribution	Europe, Africa
Length	1.1 to 1.3 in
Wingspan	Up to 5.1 in
Female color	Mainly gray, white border and eyespots
Male color	Same as female

Diet The impressive caterpillars of the giant peacock moth feed on the foliage of a range of trees, including the walnut, pear, ash and poplar.

Fact The giant peacock moth is the largest moth in Europe. The larvae are bright green in color and have a yellow stripe running along each side.

Conservation status	Not evaluated

Conservation status
(see opposite page)

Page number

Siamese rhinoceros beetle

Factfile

Each page comes with a detailed factfile containing descriptions, information, facts and figures.

Habitat
This indicates the environment that the insect lives in. Some may live in many different habitats, while others will only be able to survive in one specific habitat.

Distribution
This describes where in the world the insect is found in its natural habitat.

Diet
A description of the food that the insect eats and where it gets the food.

Length
Describes the average dimensions the insect will grow to by adulthood, given optimal conditions.

Wingspan
A measurement of the insect's wings taken from tip to tip.

Female color
A description of the color of the adult female.

Male color
A description of the color of the adult male.

Fact
Every factfile comes with an interesting fact about each insect.

Conservation status

Each animal in this book has been given a conservation status. This status indicates the threat of extinction to the species in its native home.

Not evaluated
The animals within this category have not yet been evaluated for their conservation status.

Least concern
This is the lowest risk category. Animals in this category are widespread and abundant.

Near threatened
The animals in this category are likely to become endangered in the near future.

Vulnerable
There is a high risk that animals within this category will become endangered in the wild.

Endangered
There is a high risk that animals within this category will become extinct in the wild.

Critically endangered
There is an extremely high risk of animals in this category becoming extinct in the wild.

Insect groups

The insects in this book have been categorized into eight main groups. Although the insects in each group may not all look alike, they do share some traits and characteristics.

Silverfish and springtails
Around 8,500 species

These small and primitive insects are wingless. They have flexible bodies.

Dragonflies and relatives
Around 9,000 species

These long-bodied insects have short antennae and large, multifaceted eyes. They have one or two pairs of wings which show complex patterns of veins.

The long body of the emperor dragonfly.

Cockroaches and relatives
Around 8,800 species

Cockroaches and earwigs are scavengers who eat a variety of food. Mantids are equipped with highly modified front legs used to grasp their prey.

Grasshoppers and relatives
Around 28,000 species

Most insects in this group have long hind legs designed for jumping. Many are wingless or have very small wings. Stick insects are long, slender insects with biting mouthparts.

Beetles, bugs and relatives
Over 460,000 species

Beetles have hard wing cases, called elytra, that meet in a straight line down the insect's back. The elytra are used for protection. The hind wings, if present, are folded away neatly underneath. Bugs range from tiny aphids to giant water bugs. They all have sharp mouthparts which are used to pierce and suck the juices from animals and plants.

Ladybugs have sharp biting mouthparts.

Flies
Over 150,000 species

These common insects usually have two wings that they use for flight and a second pair that they use for balancing.

Butterflies and moths
Over 165,000 species

The insects in this group all have large wings, which often have bright patterns and colors. Butterflies are active during the day, while moths are mostly active during the night.

The monarch butterfly has bright, colorful wings.

Bees, wasps and ants
Over 200,000 species

All insects in this group have chewing mouthpieces. Bees and wasps generally have two pairs of wings, whereas ants are mostly wingless.

Contents

Common Silverfish

Lepisma saccharina

Factfile

Habitat	Moist, dark areas
Distribution	Europe, Africa, the Americas, Asia, Australasia
Length	.31 to .79 in
Wingspan	Wingless
Female color	Silver
Male color	Same as female

Diet Silverfish feed on anything from flour and leftover food to glue and even clothes. They can survive for several months without eating any food.

Fact The silverfish has a silvery, scaly appearance. They are fast-moving insects who are often found under furniture or in among old books.

Conservation status   **Least concern**

Clover Springtail
Sminthurus viridis

Factfile

Habitat	Soil in grassland and woodland
Distribution	Europe, Australia
Length	.04 to .08 in
Wingspan	Wingless
Female color	Pale yellow, green or dark brown
Male color	Same as female

Diet Most springtails eat dead and decaying plants, but the clover springtail feeds mainly on live plant material, particularly plants such as clover or peas.

Fact A springtail uses a pair of appendages on the fourth abdominal segment which spring out from under its body and propel it high into the air.

Conservation status   Least concern

Broad-bodied Chaser

Libellula depressa

Factfile

Habitat	Waterside vegetation and surrounding areas
Distribution	Europe
Length	1.6 to 1.8 in
Wingspan	Up to 2.8 in
Female color	Yellow-brown abdomen with yellow edges
Male color	Pale-blue abdomen with yellow edges

Diet Gnats, midges and mosquitoes make up the bulk of the chaser's diet. If it catches larger insects it will eat the bodies and discard the wings.

Fact As adults, broad-bodied chasers do not live as long as many of the other dragonflies. Chasers sometimes live for no longer than 4 weeks.

Conservation status   **Least concern**

Common Clubtail
Gomphus vulgatissimus

Factfile

Habitat	Waterside vegetation and surrounding areas
Distribution	Europe
Length	1.8 to 2.2 in
Wingspan	Up to 2.6 in
Female color	Black abdomen with yellow stripes on thorax
Male color	As female, but stripes turn green

Diet The common clubtail eats gnats, mayflies, flies, mosquitoes and other small flying insects. Sometimes they will also eat moths, butterflies and bees.

Fact The female will either drop her eggs into water in flight or dip them onto the surface. The larvae live in sediment for 3 to 5 years before emerging.

Conservation status   **Near threatened**

Common Hawker

Aeshna juncea

Factfile

Habitat	Waterside, open country
Distribution	Europe
Length	2.8 to 3.1 in
Wingspan	Up to 3.5 in
Female color	Brown with yellow spots
Male color	Blue spots and yellow marks

Diet Hawkers are incredibly fast-flying dragonflies. They spend their adult lives flying around searching for other insects to capture and eat.

Fact The larvae of the common hawker takes 3 to 4 years to develop into an adult. Once fully developed, the adult will only survive for a few weeks.

Conservation status   **Least concern**

Emperor Dragonfly

Anax imperator

Factfile

Habitat	Waterside vegetation, open water
Distribution	Europe
Length	2.8 to 3.4 in
Wingspan	Up to 4.3 in
Female color	Green thorax, greenish-blue abdomen
Male color	Deep-blue, black-lined abdomen

Diet These dragonflies will typically catch and eat prey while in mid-flight. Large prey, such as butterflies, will be eaten from the safety of a perch.

Fact Dragonflies can fly at speeds of 31 miles per hour. This species breeds in weedy ponds and ditches. The female will lay her eggs in submerged plants.

Conservation status	**Least concern**

Green Darner

Anax junius

Factfile

Habitat Small ponds
Distribution North America, Central America
Length 2.8 to 3.1 in
Wingspan Up to 3.9 in
Female color Green, red or brown abdomen, green thorax
Male color Bright-blue abdomen, green thorax

Diet The larvae feed on aquatic invertebrates, as well as fish eggs and tadpoles. Adults consume insects, including butterflies and other dragonflies.

Fact Green darners are some of the largest dragonflies in North America. They can be found across the USA and Canada and south to Costa Rica.

Conservation status **Least concern**

Flame Skimmer

Libellula saturata

Factfile

Habitat	Lakes and ponds
Distribution	Southwest USA, Mexico
Length	2.0 to 2.4 in
Wingspan	Up to 3.1 in
Female color	Bright-red body with orange wings
Male color	Same as female

Diet The flame skimmer will eat almost any soft-bodied flying insect, including mosquitoes, butterflies, moths, mayflies, flying ants or termites.

Fact When the female lays eggs, she deposits them in various places to prevent other animals from finding all her eggs and using them all as a source of food.

Conservation status   **Least concern**

Slender Skimmer

Orthetrum sabina

Factfile

Habitat	Watercourses, ponds, drains
Distribution	Europe, Africa, Asia, Australia
Length	2.0 to 2.4 in
Wingspan	Up to 2.9 in
Female color	Pale yellow green with black stripes
Male color	Same as female

Diet The slender skimmer is a fierce predator. It is well known for attacking and feeding on other dragonflies, including some species larger than itself.

Fact When the female is ready to lay her eggs in water, she is guarded by the male. The male will attack and fight off any animal that approaches her.

Conservation status   **Least concern**

Eastern Amberwing
Perithemis tenera

Factfile

Habitat	Ponds, lakes, slow streams
Distribution	North America
Length	.79 to .98 in
Wingspan	Up to 1.2 in
Female color	Brown and yellow body, spotted amber wings
Male color	Brown and yellow body, plain amber wings

Diet Eastern amberwings eat flying insects. They often feed on insects that are considered pests to humans, such as mayflies and mosquitoes.

Fact The eastern amberwing is one of a few dragonflies who mimic the colors of deadly insects, such as wasps, in order to warn off any predators.

Conservation status	**Not evaluated**

Emerald Damselfly

Lestes sponsa

Insects

Dragonflies and relatives

Damselflies

Factfile

Habitat	Waterside vegetation
Distribution	Europe
Length	.98 to 1.4 in
Wingspan	Up to 1.7 in
Female color	Dull-green body
Male color	Bright, metallic green with a blue thorax

Diet The larvae of emerald damselflies feed on small crustaceans and insect larvae. As adults they will hunt a variety of other flying insects.

Fact The emerald damselfly can often be seen resting with its wings open. This habit has earned it the nickname "the common spreadwing."

Conservation status   **Least concern**

Large Red Damselfly

Pyrrhosoma nymphula

Factfile

Habitat	Freshwater habitats
Distribution	Europe
Length	1.4 to 1.6 in
Wingspan	Up to 2.0 in
Female color	Red abdomen with black markings
Male color	Same as female but sometimes more vibrant

Diet The large red damselfly is an expert hunter who feeds on a variety of small insects, which it will snatch from vegetation close to water.

Fact Large red damselflies, like most damselflies, rest with their wings folded along their body (unlike dragonflies, who rest with their wings open).

Conservation status　　　　　**Least concern**

Beautiful Demoiselle
Calopteryx virgo

Insects

Dragonflies and relatives

Damselflies

Factfile

Habitat	Fast rivers
Distribution	Europe
Length	1.6 to 2.0 in
Wingspan	Up to 2.6 in
Female color	Blue-green body, pale wings
Male color	Same as female

Diet The beautiful demoiselle is a voracious predator. They have superb eyesight which they use to locate and catch prey.

Fact Beautiful demoiselles are very sensitive to pollution as the larvae need water with a high oxygen content. Its presence is a sign of good water quality.

Conservation status **Least concern**

Banded Demoiselle
Calopteryx splendens

Factfile

Habitat	Slow rivers
Distribution	Europe, Asia
Length	1.6 to 2.0 in
Wingspan	Up to 2.6 in
Female color	Shiny, metallic green
Male color	Metallic blue green

Diet Like many other damselflies the banded demoiselle catches most of its prey in mid-flight. It survives on a diet of soft-bodied flying insects.

Fact The eggs take around 2 weeks to hatch. The nymphs live underwater among aquatic vegetation, usually for 2 years, before developing into adults.

Conservation status   **Least concern**

21

Common Mayfly
Ephemera danica

Insects

Dragonflies and relatives

Mayflies

Factfile

Habitat	Slow rivers and streams, lakes
Distribution	Europe
Length	.40 to 1.2 in
Wingspan	Up to 1.6 in
Female color	Cream or gray
Male color	Same as female

Diet Nymphs feed on plant material, algae and debris on rocks. Adults only live for a few days, so they have no functional mouthparts and do not feed.

Fact Mayflies fly mainly at night. The nymphs live in lakes and rivers with fine sand or silt. Nymphs take around 2 years to mature into adult mayflies.

Conservation status   **Near threatened**

Giant Cockroach
Blaberus giganteus

Factfile

Habitat	Rain forest
Distribution	Central America, northern South America
Length	2.9 to 3.9 in
Wingspan	Up to 7.0 in
Female color	Light yellow to brown
Male color	Same as female

Diet These cockroaches are scavengers. They mostly feed on decaying plant material, but will also eat bat droppings, fruit, seeds and dead animals.

Fact The giant cockroach is one of the largest cockroaches in the world. They can be found in moist dark areas such as caves and tree hollows.

Conservation status	Near threatened

Hissing Cockroach

Gromphadorhina portentosa

Factfile

Habitat	Forest floor
Distribution	Madagascar
Length	3.1 to 3.9 in
Wingspan	Wingless
Female color	Brown with dark-orange marks
Male color	Same as female

Diet The hissing cockroach scavenges at night for meals. It feeds primarily on a diet of dead animal matter, smaller insects, waste food and ripe fruit.

Fact This cockroach is one of the largest cockroaches. It is known for the hissing sound it makes by pushing air through breathing holes in its side.

Conservation status　　　　**Least concern**

Oriental Cockroach

Blatta orientalis

Factfile

Habitat	Houses, warm places
Distribution	Worldwide (except Antarctica)
Length	.70 to .87 in
Wingspan	Up to 1.2 in
Female color	Brown to black
Male color	Same as female

Diet Oriental cockroaches are omnivores, which means they eat animals and plant matter. They feed on rubbish, sewage, or decaying organic matter.

Fact A female oriental cockroach produces 6 egg capsules during her life. Each capsule holds 16 eggs. They are left near food and will hatch in 12 weeks.

Conservation status   **Least concern**

Death's Head Cockroach

Blaberus craniifer

Factfile

Habitat	Scrub, houses
Distribution	The Americas
Length	1.6 to 2.3 in
Wingspan	Up to 2.4 in
Female color	Brown and cream body
Male color	Same as female

Diet The death's head cockroach is an omnivore and will feed on anything, even feces or wood. It is able to eat half of its own weight at once.

Fact Like many other species of cockroach, the death's head can give off a very unpleasant odor when it becomes frightened or disturbed.

Conservation status   **Least concern**

Giant Burrowing Cockroach

Macropanesthia rhinoceros

Factfile

Habitat	Soil
Distribution	Australia
Length	Up to 3.1 in
Wingspan	Wingless
Female color	Shiny dark brown or black
Male color	Same as female

Diet Giant burrowing cockroaches live in rotting timber. They have a diet of dried, dead gum leaves, which they collect from the ground.

Fact This wingless cockroach is found mainly in northern Queensland, Australia. Females produce between 5 and 30 young in early summer.

Conservation status   **Least concern**

27

Praying Mantis

Mantis religiosa

Insects

Cockroaches and relatives

Mantids

Factfile

Habitat	Savannah, grassland, forest
Distribution	Africa, Europe, Asia, North America
Length	2.9 to 3.1 in
Wingspan	Up to 3.1 in
Female color	Green or brown
Male color	Same as female

Diet The praying mantis is a carnivorous predator. It will even attack small reptiles and birds. It can be cannibalistic and will sometimes eat other mantids.

Fact The most striking features on a praying mantis are the grasping front legs. These legs are well designed for grabbing and holding the insect's prey.

Conservation status   **Least concern**

Conehead Mantis

Empusa pennata

Factfile

Habitat	Vegetation, bushes, grasses
Distribution	Europe
Length	Up to 3.9 in
Wingspan	Up to 7.0 in
Female color	Brownish-green body
Male color	Same as female

Diet Like other mantids, the conehead is a carnivore that uses its strong front legs to catch and grasp insects before eating them.

Fact There are small differences between the sexes. The female has shorter wings. Males also have feathered antennae while the females' are straight.

Conservation status **Least concern**

29

Common Earwig

Forficula auricularia

Factfile

Habitat	In soil under stones
Distribution	Europe, USA
Length	.40 to .60 in
Wingspan	Up to .47 in
Female color	Reddish brown
Male color	Same as female

Diet The common earwig's diet consists of spiders, small insects, insect eggs, plants, fruits and flowers. They also scavenge and eat dead animal matter.

Fact Earwigs have pincers at the tip of their abdomens. These pincers are used for grooming, capturing prey and for folding the wings back after flight.

Conservation status   **Least concern**

Tawny Earwig

Labidura riparia

Factfile

Habitat	Ponds, lakes, seashores
Distribution	Worldwide (except Antarctica)
Length	.98 to 1.4 in
Wingspan	Up to .79 in
Female color	Yellowish brown to dark blackish brown
Male color	Same as female

Diet The tawny earwig eats invertebrates, including aphids, maggots and beetle larvae. They may occasionally feed on some plant material.

Fact The tawny earwig has many other names including the giant earwig, striped earwig, riparian earwig, and common brown earwig.

Conservation status   **Least concern**

Blue-winged Grasshopper

Oedipoda caerulescens

Factfile

Habitat	Dry, stony and sandy areas
Distribution	Europe, North Africa, Asia
Length	.60 to 1.2 in
Wingspan	Up to 1.1 in
Female color	Brown and gray body, bright-blue hind wings
Male color	Same as female

Diet Most grasshoppers are herbivores, meaning they only eat plants. They eat a variety of different grasses, leaves and some cereal crops.

Fact The bright-blue hind wings of this grasshopper are only ever seen when it is in flight. It can often be mistaken for a butterfly when flying.

Conservation status   **Least concern**

Common Field Grasshopper

Chorthippus brunneus

Factfile

Habitat	Dry grassland
Distribution	Europe, Asia, North Africa
Length	.60 to .98 in
Wingspan	Up to .98 in
Female color	Usually brown
Male color	Same as female

Diet The common field grasshopper is a herbivore. It will eat almost any type of leaf, but prefers soft vegetation. The majority of its diet is grass.

Fact When grasshoppers are picked up, they "spit" a brown liquid commonly called "tobacco juice." This liquid may protect them from predators.

Conservation status   **Least concern**

Meadow Grasshopper

Chorthippus parallelus

Factfile

Habitat	Grassland
Distribution	Europe
Length	.60 to .79 in
Wingspan	.87 to .98 in
Female color	Greenish brown or even purplish
Male color	Greenish brown

Diet These grasshoppers are strict herbivores. They eat grasses, weeds, leaves, shrubs, bark and many of the other plants that surround them.

Fact To attract a mate, the male can be seen displaying to females by rubbing its legs against its wings to create a "song" – a regular "rrrr" sound.

Conservation status **Least concern**

34

Migratory Locust

Locusta migratoria

Factfile

Habitat	Grassland
Distribution	Europe, Africa, Asia, Australia, New Zealand
Length	2.2 to 2.6 in
Wingspan	Up to 3.1 in
Female color	From brown and green to greenish yellow
Male color	Same as female

Diet Migratory locusts feed on a limited number of plants, preferring wild grasses. Each individual eats 10.5 to 17.5 ounces of green foliage during its life.

Fact In Africa, populations of migratory locusts can grow to groups of millions. Large groups like this can destroy farm crops and strip vegetation.

Conservation status   **Least concern**

Mole Cricket
Gryllotalpa gryllotalpa

Factfile

Habitat	Sandy or peaty soil
Distribution	Europe, western Asia, North Africa
Length	1.4 to 1.8 in
Wingspan	Up to 1.2 in
Female color	Brown body
Male color	Same as female

Diet Mole crickets are omnivorous, feeding on a range of soil invertebrates and plant roots. They leave neat circular holes in the roots of tuberous plants.

Fact Adults and nymphs can be found throughout the year in underground tunnel systems. These tunnels may reach a depth of over 3 feet.

Conservation status   **Least concern**

Great Green Bush Cricket

Tettigonia viridissima

Factfile

Habitat	Dry grassland
Distribution	Europe, Africa, Asia, Australia, New Zealand
Length	1.4 to 1.7 in
Wingspan	Up to 2.4 in
Female color	Mainly green with brown stripe on back
Male color	Same as female

Diet The great green bush cricket eats soft-bodied invertebrates such as flies, caterpillars and larvae. It has strong jaws able to inflict a nasty bite.

Fact Like the gecko, the great green bush cricket has "sticky" feet. It can walk on smooth vertical surfaces, and even upside down, with no trouble.

Conservation status   **Least concern**

Predatory Bush Cricket

Saga pedo

Factfile

Habitat	Dry scrub, grassland
Distribution	Europe
Length	6.0 to 6.7 in
Wingspan	Wingless
Female color	Bright green
Male color	No males

Diet Predatory bush crickets feed on grasshoppers, locusts and some mantids. Like other *Saga* species they are known to have cannibalistic tendencies.

Fact The entire population consists of females. Reproduction relies on parthenogenesis, where unfertilized eggs develop into "clones" of the mother.

Conservation status | **Vulnerable**

True Katydid

Pterophylla camellifolia

Factfile

Habitat	Trees, bushes
Distribution	North America
Length	1.7 to 1.9 in
Wingspan	Up to 1.6 in
Female color	Leafy green
Male color	Same as female

Diet The true katydid is a herbivore. It eats the foliage of deciduous trees and shrubs. Females glue their eggs underneath the leaves of the trees they eat.

Fact Unlike grasshoppers and crickets, both male and female katydids make sounds. They rub their forewings together to "sing" to each other.

Conservation status   **Least concern**

Northern Walkingstick

Diapheromera femorata

Insects

Grasshoppers and relatives

Stick Insects

Factfile

Habitat	Forest
Distribution	North America
Length	3.0 to 3.7 in
Wingspan	Wingless
Female color	Greenish brown
Male color	Light brown

Diet The northern walkingstick eats the leaves of trees, including oak, sassafras, black cherry and the black locust tree. They will also eat clover.

Fact Females drop eggs onto the forest floor. The eggs stay in leaf litter and hatch in the spring. They develop into adults in the summer and autumn.

Conservation status **Least concern**

40

Twenty-two Spot Ladybug

Psyllobora vigintiduopunctata

Factfile

Habitat	Low vegetation
Distribution	Europe
Length	.12 to .20 in
Wingspan	Up to .31 in
Female color	Yellow (or white) with black spots
Male color	Same as female

Diet The twenty-two spot ladybug is unusual among ladybugs as it eats mildew. It grazes for food from the soil surface or from low vegetation.

Fact The twenty-two spot ladybug is one of the brightest of the yellow ladybugs. The spots very rarely join up. It is also one of the smallest ladybugs.

Conservation status   **Least concern**

Seven-spot Ladybug

Coccinella septempunctata

Factfile

Habitat	Gardens, meadows, fields
Distribution	Europe
Length	.21 to .31 in
Wingspan	Up to .60 in
Female color	Red (or occasionally yellow) with black spots
Male color	Same as female

Diet The seven-spot ladybug has a diet of insects, such as aphids. They are popular with gardeners and farmers as they help protect plants and crops.

Fact They have red wing cases with 7 spots, although some may have more or fewer spots. They hibernate for the winter months in cracks and crevices.

Conservation status   Least concern

Harlequin Ladybug

harmonia axyridis

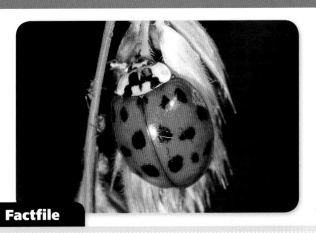

Factfile

Habitat	Parks, gardens
Distribution	Asia, Europe, North America
Length	.24 to .31 in
Wingspan	Up to .47 in
Female color	Reddish orange and black
Male color	Same as female

Diet Harlequin ladybugs have a diet consisting of invertebrates, including butterflies and lacewings. It will also eat other ladybugs smaller than itself.

Fact The harlequin ladybug is sometimes called the Asian ladybug because it was introduced from Asia to other areas to control aphids.

Conservation status   Least concern

Cream-spot Ladybug

Calvia quatuordecimguttata

Factfile

Habitat	Savannah, grassland, forest
Distribution	North America, Europe, Asia
Length	.14 to .21 in
Wingspan	Up to .24 in
Female color	Black or orange red with cream spots
Male color	Same as female

Diet Cream-spot ladybugs, like most ladybugs, are insectivores. This means that they only eat other insects. They thrive on a diet of psyllids and aphids.

Fact Cream-spot ladybugs usually have 14 spots. The spots can vary in size and shape. The background color may be black or orange red.

Conservation status   **Least concern**

44

Green Tiger Beetle
Cicindela campestris

Factfile

Habitat	Sandy areas of heath, hillside and dune
Distribution	Europe, Asia
Length	.41 to .57 in
Wingspan	Up to 1.2 in
Female color	Bright metallic green
Male color	Same as female

Diet Green tiger beetles are fast-moving beetles. They are pure predators, and feed on any smaller insect or spider that they happen to spot.

Fact Green tiger beetles have powerful jaws. Once they have located and captured their prey, they use their jaws to tear it into many pieces.

Conservation status   **Least concern**

Blue-spotted Tiger Beetle

Cicindela aurulenta

Factfile

Habitat	Forest, sand dunes, mangrove
Distribution	Asia
Length	.70 to .87 in
Wingspan	Up to 1.2 in
Female color	Iridescent blue green, yellow or orange
Male color	Same as female

Diet The blue-spotted tiger beetle, like all tiger beetles, is a fast-running predator that feeds on small insects, spiders, and other arthropods.

Fact The larvae of the blue-spotted tiger beetle live hidden in burrows with their jaws at surface level, ready to grab any insect that wanders too close.

Conservation status **Not evaluated**

Blue Ground Beetle
Carabus intricatus

Factfile

Habitat	Woodland
Distribution	Europe, Asia
Length	.98 to 1.5 in
Wingspan	Wingless
Female color	Metallic purple or blue
Male color	Same as female

Diet Blue ground beetles are carnivores and hunt during the dark of night. Recent studies have discovered that their favorite food is the tree slug.

Fact This beetle takes 2 years to complete its life cycle from egg to fully grown adult. The adults live for a very long time compared to most beetles.

Conservation status	Near threatened

Violet Ground Beetle

Carabus violaceus

Factfile

Habitat	Soil
Distribution	Europe, Asia
Length	.79 to 1.2 in
Wingspan	Wingless
Female color	Dark with violet tinge around body
Male color	Same as female

Diet
Violet ground beetles are most active at night. The adults and larvae both hunt and feed on slugs, snails, worms and a variety of other insects.

Fact
When disturbed the violet ground beetle can exude a nasty-smelling fluid from its abdomen. This will often deter any predator from attacking.

Conservation status	**Least concern**

Black Oil Beetle

Meloe proscarabaeus

Factfile

Habitat	Low-lying flat terrain
Distribution	Europe
Length	.43 to .98 in
Wingspan	Wingless
Female color	Bluish black
Male color	Same as female

Diet The larvae of the black oil beetle (known as tringulins) feed on the pollen stores and eggs that are found in the burrows of ground bees.

Fact Oil beetles get their name from the smelly oil that they are able to produce from their legs. This oil helps to dissuade predators from eating them.

Conservation status   **Vulnerable**

Emerald Ash Borer

Agrilus planipenni

Factfile

Habitat	Ash trees
Distribution	Asia, North America
Length	Up to .75 in
Wingspan	Up to 1.4 in
Female color	Green with multicolored thorax
Male color	Dark metallic green

Diet The adult beetles eat foliage from ash trees. Larvae feed on the inner bark of ash trees, disrupting the tree's ability to transport water and nutrients.

Fact These beetles arrived in North America in the wood of pallets on ships. Since arriving they have caused millions of dollars of damage to ash trees.

Conservation status   **Least concern**

Tanbark Borer

Phymatodes testaceus

Factfile

Habitat	Areas with dead timber
Distribution	Europe, Asia, North America
Length	.31 to .51 in
Wingspan	Up to .87 in
Female color	Golden brown, reddish, or blue black
Male color	Same as female

Diet The tanbark borer feeds on wood, oak in particular. These longhorn beetles can often be brought into people's houses inside firewood.

Fact Eggs are laid under the bark of standing dead timber or recently cut trunks, with oak being the main host, although several other species are used.

Conservation status	Least concern

Great Diving Beetle

Dytiscus marginalis

Factfile

Habitat	Aquatic habitats, both still and running water
Distribution	Europe, Northern Asia
Length	1.1 to 1.4 in
Wingspan	Up to 2.0 in
Female color	Dark brown to blackish with yellow legs
Male color	Same as female

Diet Great diving beetles are aquatic predators. They eat fish and tadpoles. They hunt prey by diving through zones in the water where light reaches.

Fact Diving beetles carry air under their wing cases. They do this so they are able to dive for a longer time without returning to the surface to breathe.

Conservation status	Least concern

Cereal Leaf Beetle

Oulema melanopus

Factfile

Habitat	Fields, grassland, agricultural areas
Distribution	Europe, Africa, USA, Canada
Length	.20 to .24 in
Wingspan	Up to .40 in
Female color	Dark body with green sheen, red head
Male color	Same as female

Diet Cereal leaf beetles can be pests to farmers. Their larvae eat green tissue between the leaf veins, while adults eat barley, oat and wheat crops.

Fact The larvae of cereal leaf beetles are slug-like. They are covered in a sticky, yellowish-gray secretion. The skin is yellowish and the head brown.

Conservation status	**Least concern**

Devil's Coach Horse Beetle

Ocypus olens

Insects

Beetles, bugs and relatives

Beetles

Factfile

Habitat	Forest, parks, gardens
Distribution	Europe, the Americas, Australasia
Length	.87 to 1.3 in
Wingspan	Up to .63 in
Female color	Dark body
Male color	Same as female

Diet The devil's coach horse beetle preys on other invertebrates at night. It eats insects, woodlice and slugs, and also feeds on any dead animals it finds.

Fact When a devil's coach horse beetle feels threatened it produces a nasty-smelling chemical from a pair of glands found on its abdomen.

Conservation status   **Least concern**

Colorado Potato Beetle
Leptinotarsa decemlineata

Factfile

Habitat	Farm fields, grassland
Distribution	North America, Europe, Asia
Length	.31 to .40 in
Wingspan	Up to .79 in
Female color	Yellow or orange body with brown stripes
Male color	Same as female

Diet The Colorado potato beetle feeds on solanum plants, such as potato plants. It eats most parts of the plant, leaving only the roots and stems.

Fact Farmers find it very difficult to control Colorado potato beetles, as they breed quickly and can also become immune to conventional insecticides.

Conservation status   **Least concern**

55

Flightless Dung Beetle

Circellium bacchus

Insects

Beetles, bugs and relatives

Beetles

Factfile

Habitat	Desert, farmland, forest, grassland
Distribution	Worldwide (except Antarctica)
Length	.04 to 2.4 in
Wingspan	Wingless
Female color	Mostly dark colored
Male color	Same as female

Diet Dung beetles eat dung, the waste from other animals. The larvae and young beetles eat the solid dung, while adults drink the liquids of the dung.

Fact Dung beetles can be seen as nature's waste control. By eating and burying dung these beetles are helping to recycle nutrients into the soil.

Conservation status   **Near threatened**

Fiddler Beetle

Eupoecila australasiae

Factfile

Habitat	Heath, woodland
Distribution	Australia
Length	.60 to .70 in
Wingspan	Up to 1.2 in
Female color	Shiny black, bright yellow-green markings
Male color	Same as female

Diet Adult fiddler beetles eat nectar and pollen from flowers, and occasionally leaves. The larvae of these beetles feed on rotten wood in the soil.

Fact Fiddler beetles have striking violin-shaped markings on their backs. The female lays her eggs in rotting wood or damp ground near food sources.

Conservation status   **Least concern**

Hercules Beetle

Dynastes hercules

Factfile

Habitat	Tropical rain forest
Distribution	Central America, South America
Length	1.6 to 6.7 in
Wingspan	Up to 7.0 in
Female color	Black, brown, green, blue, white, or yellow
Male color	Same as female

Diet Rotting wood is one of the favorite meals of the Hercules beetle. They also eat fruit and other plant matter as well as the occasional small insect.

Fact The Hercules beetle is one of the largest beetles in the world. The male has enormous horn-like pincers, which protrude from his forehead.

Conservation status   **Near threatened**

Eastern Hercules Beetle

Dynastes tityus

Factfile

Habitat	Woodland
Distribution	North America
Length	2.2 to 2.5 in
Wingspan	Up to 3.5 in
Female color	Green, gray or tan, with black mottling
Male color	Same as female

Diet Although these large beetles look ferocious, they are harmless herbivores that feed mainly on fruit and sap. The larvae feed on rotting wood.

Fact The larvae of the eastern Hercules beetle are eaten by mammals, including skunks and raccoons, and arthropods, such as centipedes and spiders.

Conservation status   Not evaluated

Japanese Beetle

Popillia japonica

Factfile

Habitat	Forest, grassland, farms, cities, gardens
Distribution	East Asia, North America
Length	.40 to .47 in
Wingspan	Up to .60 in
Female color	Metallic body and bronze wing covers
Male color	Same as female

Diet These beetles feed on the flowers, fruit and leaves of plants and trees such as grape, peach, rose, cherry, soybean, hibiscus, Indian mallow and willow.

Fact Japanese beetles travel and feed in groups. Swarms have been known to strip a peach tree in 15 minutes, leaving behind only branches.

Conservation status   Least concern

June Beetle
Phyllophaga

Factfile

Habitat	Savannah, grassland, agricultural areas
Distribution	Europe, the Americas, Africa, Asia
Length	.47 to .63 in
Wingspan	Up to .94 in
Female color	Reddish brown
Male color	Same as female

Diet Adult June beetles feed on foliage and flowers at night. The larvae, called white grubs, can destroy crops, lawns and pastures by eating the roots.

Fact The larvae live underground for 3 years eating roots before they develop fully. As adults they live above ground for less than 1 year.

Conservation status   **Least concern**

Caterpillar Hunter

Calosoma scrutator

Insects

Beetles, bugs and relatives

Beetles

Factfile

Habitat	Woodland floor, rocks, decaying wood
Distribution	North America
Length	.98 to 1.4 in
Wingspan	Up to 1.4 in
Female color	Metallic green with red margins on wing cases
Male color	Same as female

Diet Caterpillar hunters climb trees to find caterpillars to feed on. They play an important role in keeping caterpillar numbers under control.

Fact These beetles survive for up to 3 years. They can emit a foul-smelling fluid as a form of self-defense. This acidic fluid can blister human skin.

Conservation status   **Not evaluated**

Forest Caterpillar Hunter

Calosoma sycophanta

Factfile

Habitat	Forest
Distribution	Central Europe, Asia, North America
Length	.98 to 1.2 in
Wingspan	1.4 to 1.8 in
Female color	Golden green with a dark-blue thorax
Male color	Same as female

Diet The forest caterpillar hunter feeds on tent caterpillars, gypsy moth caterpillars and pupae, cankerworms, cutworms, and various other caterpillars.

Fact The forest caterpillar hunter is a native to Europe and Asia. In 1901 it was introduced to the USA in order to control outbreaks of gypsy moths.

Conservation status   **Least concern**

Dogbane Leaf Beetle

Chrysochus auratus

Insects

Beetles, bugs and relatives

Beetles

Factfile

Habitat	Savannah, grassland, forest
Distribution	North America
Length	.31 to .43 in
Wingspan	Up to .63 in
Female color	Iridescent blue green with a copper shine
Male color	Same as female

Diet Dogbane leaf beetles feed mostly on dogbane plants, specifically Indian hemp and spreading dogbane. They also like to feed on milkweed.

Fact After they have fed on the low-latex tissue part of a leaf, they place their mouthparts on the leaf and walk backward in order to rub the latex off.

Conservation status	**Near threatened**

Asian Longhorned Beetle

Anoplophora glabripennis

Factfile

Habitat	Forest, urban, suburban, agricultural
Distribution	China, Korea, some of North America
Length	.79 to 1.4 in
Wingspan	Up to 2.0 in
Female color	Glossy black with white marks on wing covers
Male color	Same as female

Diet As adults, Asian longhorneds feed on leaves, twigs and other plant matter. Juvenile beetles eat the bark and tissue from hardwood trees.

Fact Asian longhorneds take up to 2 years to develop from egg to adult. Females chew grooves in the bark of a tree and lay an egg in each groove.

Conservation status   **Least concern**

Stag Beetle

Lucanus cervus

Factfile

Habitat   Woodland, gardens
Distribution Africa, Asia, Australia, Europe, the Americas
Length   1.4 to 2.9 in
Wingspan   Up to 2.4 in
Female color Black and reddish brown
Male color   Same as female

Diet Stag beetle larvae eat rotting wood. They take a long time to mature as their food is not very nutritious. Adults feed on the sap from trees.

Fact Male stag beetles have large mandibles (jaws), which look like antlers. Females don't have such big jaws but theirs are actually much stronger.

Conservation status   **Least concern**

Deathwatch Beetle

Xestobium rufovillosum

Factfile

Habitat	Areas with dead timber
Distribution	Europe, northern Asia
Length	.20 to .35 in
Wingspan	Up to .47 in
Female color	Reddish to dark brown
Male color	Same as female

Diet Deathwatch larvae eat fungi in damp timber. Adult beetles bore holes into soft woods and occasionally plaster, textiles and even books.

Fact Deathwatch beetles can cause damage to buildings. They lay eggs on wood and the larvae tunnel through the wood. This can cause structural damage.

Conservation status   Least concern

Poplar Leaf Beetle

Chrysomela populi

Factfile

Habitat	Trees and bushes
Distribution	Europe
Length	.04 to .47 in
Wingspan	Up to .60 in
Female color	Blackish body with shiny red wing covers
Male color	Same as female

Diet The poplar leaf beetle mostly eats the leaves from the poplar tree. Larvae live on the leaves and cause considerable damage to leaf tissues.

Fact The poplar leaf beetle is often found on or around poplar trees, but it is also often seen on willows, usually on the leaves or shoots.

Conservation status   **Least concern**

Burying Beetle

Nicrophorus investigator

Factfile

Habitat	Soil
Distribution	Europe, Asia, North America
Length	.47 to .70 in
Wingspan	Up to .63 in
Female color	Black with orange-red bands
Male color	Same as female

Diet The burying beetle helps to recycle nature's nutrients. It feeds on carrion and fungi, helping to dispose of the bodies of dead animals.

Fact Burying beetles have a very good sense of smell. Research has shown that they are able to smell a carcass from a distance of up to 1.8 miles away.

Conservation status   **Not evaluated**

69

Timberman Beetle

Acanthocinus aedilis

Factfile

Habitat	Pine trees
Distribution	Europe, Asia
Length	.70 to .87 in
Wingspan	Up to 1.2 in
Female color	Gray brown with brown spots
Male color	Same as female

Diet Larvae feed on rotted pine wood. A fully grown timberman will feed on a variety of foodstuffs such as pollen, nectar, leaves and wood.

Fact The timberman has very long antennae. In males the antennae are three times the body length, in females they are twice the body length.

Conservation status   **Not evaluated**

Dor Beetle

Geotrupes stercorarius

Factfile

Habitat   Woodland, meadow, farmland
Distribution   Europe, Asia, Africa
Length   .55 to .79 in
Wingspan   Up to .94 in
Female color   Shiny and black or blue back
Male color   Same as female

Diet Adult dor beetles feed on a range of food, including dung and fungi. The adults bury pieces of dung into which the female will lay eggs.

Fact Dor beetles are often found on farmland. They are important to the ecosystem as their larvae feed on dung which helps to recycle animal waste.

Conservation status   **Least concern**

Common Glow Worm

Lampyris noctiluca

Factfile

Habitat	Hedges and banks
Distribution	Europe, Asia
Length	.40 to .47 in
Wingspan	Up to .70 in (male only)
Female color	Gray brown
Male color	Same as female

Diet Glow worm larvae are fierce predators. They search leaf litter for snails and slugs. They paralyze prey then liquefy and suck the prey empty.

Fact The grub-like female can emit a greenish-yellow light from 3 segments of her abdomen. She uses her ability to glow as a way of attracting males.

Conservation status   Not evaluated

Green Carab Beetle

Calosoma schayeri

Factfile

Habitat	Forest, urban areas
Distribution	Australia
Length	.87 to 1.0 in
Wingspan	Up to 1.9 in
Female color	Iridescent green
Male color	Same as female

Diet Green carab beetles eat slow-moving prey such as caterpillars. They are popular with farmers as they eat pests like armyworms and cutworms.

Fact When handled this beetle gives off an unpleasant smell. At night they can often be seen swarming in large numbers around streetlights.

Conservation status	**Not evaluated**

Siamese Rhinoceros Beetle

Xylotrupes gideon

Factfile

Habitat	Jungle, forest, urban areas
Distribution	Asia, Australia
Length	1.8 to 2.4 in
Wingspan	Up to 2.6 in
Female color	Dark red, dark brown, or black
Male color	Same as female

Diet The Siamese rhinoceros beetle helps to keep the jungle environment clean by eating plants and rotting fruit that have fallen to the ground.

Fact There are over 300 species of rhinoceros beetles. The name comes from the male's "horn," which points forward from the center of the thorax.

Conservation status Not evaluated

Large Pine Weevil
Hylobius abietis

Factfile

Habitat	Conifers
Distribution	Europe
Length	.33 to .43 in
Wingspan	Up to .47 in
Female color	Black with yellow spots
Male color	Same as female

Diet The large pine weevil gnaws holes in the bark of shoots, especially on young trees. If these weevils attack a tree they can cause it to die.

Fact The breeding season for these weevils is between March and September. The 8-week larval feeding period allows for two generations each year.

Conservation status	Not evaluated

Giraffe Weevil

Trachelophorus giraffa

Factfile

Habitat	Forest
Distribution	Madagascar
Length	3.1 to 3.2 in
Wingspan	Up to 1.7 in
Female color	Shiny black with red wing cases
Male color	Same as female

Diet Adult giraffe weevils feed on the giraffe beetle tree. The weevils will spend most of their lives on these trees and rarely venture far from them.

Fact Male and female giraffe weevils have very similar coloring, but the male's neck is 2 to 3 times longer than that of the female.

Conservation status	**Not evaluated**

Pond Skater

Gerris lacustris

Factfile

Habitat	Ponds, still water
Distribution	Europe
Length	.70 to .90 in
Wingspan	Mostly wingless
Female color	Brown or dark gray
Male color	Same as female

Diet Pond skaters mainly feed on insects that fall into the water. They also eat aquatic insects that come to the water's surface to breathe.

Fact Pond skaters have long legs, which end in a water-repellent pad of hair. This helps them move over water without breaking through the surface.

Conservation status   **Least concern**

Water Scorpion
Nepa cinerea

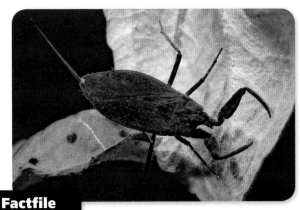

Factfile

Habitat	Ponds, lakes, dikes, streams
Distribution	Europe
Length	.70 to .87 in
Wingspan	.98 to 1.4 in
Female color	Grayish-brown upper body
Male color	Same as female

Diet A water scorpion hides in leaves until prey such as tadpoles and small fish are spotted. It will then grab the prey with its pincer-like front legs.

Fact The most notable feature of the water scorpion is the "tail." This thin projection from the rear of the insect is used as a siphon to take in air.

Conservation status	**Least concern**

Common Backswimmer
Notonecta glauca

Factfile

Habitat	Freshwater
Distribution	Europe
Length	.55 to .67 in
Wingspan	Up to .79 in
Female color	Light brown with reddish eyes
Male color	Same as female

Diet The backswimmer searches for aquatic life using its large eyes. Prey includes other insects, their larvae, tadpoles and even very small fish.

Fact The common backswimmer swims upside down. Its back is boat-shaped and it rows itself along through the water using its hind legs.

Conservation status   **Least concern**

Common Water Strider

Gerris remigis

Factfile

Habitat	Ponds, streams
Distribution	Worldwide (except Antarctica)
Length	.40 to .47 in
Wingspan	Wingless
Female color	Dark brown to black
Male color	Same as female

Diet The common water strider feeds on mosquito larvae, dead insects and other insects that accidentally fall onto the water's surface.

Fact Water striders live on the surface of the water. Their thin legs have tiny hairs that allow them to rest on the surface without breaking through.

Conservation status   **Least concern**

Aphid
Aphidoidea

Factfile

Habitat	Tender plant stems, leaves, buds
Distribution	Worldwide (except Antarctica)
Length	.12 to .20 in
Wingspan	Up to .31 in
Female color	Green
Male color	Same as female

Diet An aphid will use its long mouthparts to pierce holes in plants, and then extract the juices from the roots and stems, as well as the leaves.

Fact Aphids make a substance called honeydew from the undigested plant sugar they eat. Ants eat this honeydew and will protect the aphids.

Conservation status   **Least concern**

Green Shield Bug

Palomena Prasina

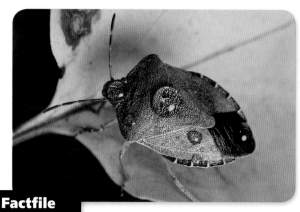

Factfile

Habitat	Shrubs in gardens, woods and parks
Distribution	Europe, North America
Length	.35 to .47 in
Wingspan	Up to .55 in
Female color	Green with brown patch on back end
Male color	Same as female

Diet The green shield bug will feed on sap from flowers, leaves and fruits. In some countries they can destroy valuable vegetable crops, as well as many plants.

Fact Shield bugs are also called stink bugs. Glands on their undersides secrete a foul-smelling fluid that helps to protect them from predators.

Conservation status	Least concern

Common Green Capsid
Lygocoris pabulinus

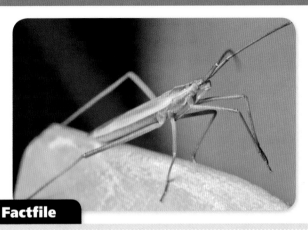

Factfile

Habitat	Trees, bushes
Distribution	Europe
Length	.20 to .24 in
Wingspan	Up to .31 in
Female color	Bright green
Male color	Same as female

Diet The common green capsid is a pest to farmers and gardeners as it sucks up the sap from shoot tips and buds, causing damage to plants.

Fact Females lay as many as 100 eggs. The eggs survive winter and then hatch as nymphs in the spring. There are normally two generations per year.

Conservation status   **Least concern**

Fine Streaked Bugkin

Miris striatus

Factfile

Habitat	Trees, bushes
Distribution	Europe, Central Asia
Length	.40 to .47 in
Wingspan	Up to .60 in
Female color	Black with yellow and orange marks on wings
Male color	Same as female

Diet The fine streaked bugkin lives on trees and bushes, especially oak and elm. It eats young leaves, small caterpillars and other soft-bodied insects.

Fact The female bugkin lays her eggs in the bark of deciduous trees, where they will overwinter. During the spring they will hatch into nymphs.

Conservation status **Least concern**

Cicada
Cicada orni

Factfile

Habitat	Trees, bushes
Distribution	Europe, Africa
Length	1.4 to 1.6 in
Wingspan	Up to 3.1 in
Female color	Mottled grayish brown
Male color	Same as female

Diet Adult cicadas are seen during the summer feeding on sap from trees or shrubs. Their mouthparts are well adapted for piercing and sucking.

Fact While their lifespan as adults is about 6 weeks, the larvae will live underground for several years, feeding on the juices from plant roots.

Conservation status	**Least concern**

Periodical Cicada

Magicicada

Insects

Beetles, bugs and relatives

Bugs

Factfile

Habitat	Woodland
Distribution	North America
Length	1.6 to 1.9 in
Wingspan	Up to 2.8 in
Female color	Dark body, red eyes and transparent wings
Male color	Same as female

Diet The adult periodical cicada will drink sap from trees to keep hydrated. While underground the nymphs will feed on the roots of trees and plants.

Fact The periodical cicada has a strange life cycle. Nymphs can spend 13 or 17 years developing underground before emerging as adults.

Conservation status   **Near threatened**

Green Coneheaded Planthopper

Acanalonia conica

Factfile

Habitat	Trees, shrubs
Distribution	North America
Length	.31 to .47 in
Wingspan	Up to .60 in
Female color	Leaf green
Male color	Same as female

Diet The green coneheaded planthopper feeds on a wide variety of native and cultivated trees, shrubs, herbaceous plants and grasses.

Fact To avoid being eaten by insect-eating animals such as birds, these planthoppers have evolved to be very well camouflaged on plant twigs.

Conservation status   **Least concern**

Giant Mesquite Bug

Thasus neocalifornicus

Factfile

Habitat	Mesquite trees
Distribution	North America
Length	1.2 to 1.6 in
Wingspan	Up to 3.1 in
Female color	Mainly red, white and gray
Male color	Same as female

Diet These bugs eat from the mesquite tree. They suck sap from the shoots and attack the leaves and seed pods. They cause no significant damage.

Fact The males have extra-large hind legs with bumps and spines. The females have thin, smooth hind legs. They gather in large groups on the trees.

Conservation status   **Not evaluated**

Harlequin Bug
Murgantia histrionica

Factfile

Habitat	Vegetable crops
Distribution	North America
Length	.31 to .47 in
Wingspan	Up to .60 in
Female color	Yellow and greenish black or red and black
Male color	Same as female

Diet Harlequin bugs suck fluids from plant tissue and leave yellow or white blotches where they have fed. Infestations often cause crops to die.

Fact The harlequin bug is a pest to cabbage, cauliflower and related crops, and it is a minor pest to other crops, including potatoes and tomatoes.

Conservation status　　　**Least concern**

Large Milkweed Bug

Oncopeltus fasciatus

Factfile

Habitat	Fields
Distribution	North America
Length	.40 to .70 in
Wingspan	Up to 1.2 in
Female color	Orange red and black
Male color	Same as female

Diet Groups of large milkweed bugs can be found feeding on common milkweed plants. It will eat this plant at all stages of its development.

Fact The bright colors of the large milkweed bug warn potential predators that they taste bad. Their bodies store toxins from the milkweed plant.

Conservation status — **Least concern**

Green Lacewing
Chrysopidae

Factfile

Habitat	Woodland, farms, gardens
Distribution	North America, Europe
Length	.70 to .98 in
Wingspan	Up to 2.6 in
Female color	Green with golden or reddish eyes
Male color	Same as female

Diet Green lacewings feed on a huge variety of insects. They are especially fond of insects with soft bodies, such as caterpillars and aphids.

Fact Lacewings are bred in large numbers in captivity. They are sometimes released onto farmland to help reduce the number of crop-eating pests.

Conservation status   **Least concern**

Bluebottle Fly

Calliphora vomitoria

Insects

Flies

Blow flies

Factfile

Habitat   Woodland, gardens, houses, urban areas
Distribution   Europe, Asia, Africa, North America
Length   .35 to .47 in
Wingspan   Up to .79 in
Female color   Blue black with red eyes
Male color   Same as female

Diet The bluebottle fly gets its food from dead animals or meat, living animals with open wounds, animal dung, or other decaying matter.

Fact Female bluebottle flies sometimes lay eggs in the wound of a living animal. The larvae, when they hatch, will begin to eat from the host animal.

Conservation status	Least concern

Housefly
Musca domestica

Factfile

Habitat	Houses
Distribution	Worldwide (except Antarctica)
Length	.31 to .40 in
Wingspan	Up to .79 in
Female color	Dark gray with red eyes
Male color	Same as female

Diet The housefly can only eat liquids. In order to liquidize solid food, the fly vomits saliva and digestive juices onto the food and then sucks it back up!

Fact The housefly is one of the most common animals in the world. It is known to spread many diseases including salmonella, anthrax and polio.

Conservation status	**Least concern**

Common Crane Fly

Tipulidae

Factfile

Habitat	Grassland, gardens
Distribution	Europe, USA
Length	1.2 to 2.4 in
Wingspan	Up to 2.6 in
Female color	Brown
Male color	Same as female

Diet The larvae of the common crane fly feed on roots of grasses and other vegetation. The adult crane fly feeds on nectar or not at all.

Fact The common crane fly is sometimes called a daddy long legs. They have slender bodies and very long and delicate legs that can easily break off.

Conservation status	**Least concern**

Mydas Fly
Mydas clavatus

Factfile

Habitat	Open country
Distribution	North America
Length	.40 to 2.4 in
Wingspan	Up to 2.0 in
Female color	Black body with orange base to the abdomen
Male color	Same as female

Diet The larvae of mydas flies feed on beetle grubs in decaying wood. The adults have a fairly short life and feed on nectar and pollen from flowers.

Fact Mydas flies can be found in various habitats but they are more often seen in open country. Females dig into the soil and lay their eggs.

Conservation status	**Not evaluated**

Common House Mosquito

Culex pipiens

Insects

Flies

Mosquitoes

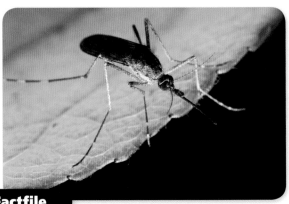

Factfile

Habitat	Near slow-moving or still water
Distribution	Europe, the Americas, Asia, Africa
Length	Up to .31 in
Wingspan	Up to .40 in
Female color	Black or brown
Male color	Same as female

Diet
The female mosquito has to drink animals' blood to lay her eggs. She uses her sharp mouthparts to pierce the victim's skin and sucks up the blood!

Fact
In hot countries mosquitoes spread deadly diseases such as malaria and dengue fever. Only the female anopheles mosquito carries malaria.

Conservation status	**Least concern**

Painted Lady Butterfly
Vanessa cardui

Factfile

Habitat	Forest, woodland, parks, mountains
Distribution	Africa, Asia, Australia, Europe, the Americas
Length	.70 to .87 in
Wingspan	Up to 2.2 in
Female color	Black, brown and orange
Male color	Same as female

Diet The caterpillars feed mostly on thistle plants. Adults will eat the nectar from flowers, such as aster, cosmos, ironweed and joe-pye weed.

Fact The painted lady is one of the best-known butterflies in the world. They are most often seen in areas across Asia, Europe and North America.

Conservation status   **Least concern**

Apollo Butterfly

Parnassius apollo

Insects

Butterflies and moths

Butterflies

Factfile

Habitat	Hilly regions
Distribution	Europe, Asia
Length	1.4 to 1.8 in
Wingspan	Up to 3.9 in
Female color	Cream with black, red and yellow markings
Male color	Same as female

Diet The caterpillars of Apollo butterflies feed mostly on stonecrop plants, while the adults feed on the nectar from flowers such as the thistle.

Fact Apollo butterflies are found in the hilly regions of Europe and Asia. Some of these butterflies live in areas as high as 2.4 miles above sea level.

Conservation status   **Vulnerable**

Common Brimstone

Gonepteryx rhamni

Factfile

Habitat	Woodland, scrub
Distribution	Europe, North Africa
Length	.98 to 1.4 in
Wingspan	Up to 2.4 in
Female color	Greenish white with orange spots
Male color	Same as female

Diet The caterpillars of the brimstone butterfly feed on buckthorn and alder buckthorn leaves, while the adult butterflies drink nectar from flowers.

Fact The female brimstone lays her eggs on leaves. The eggs are laid in May, the larvae pupate in June and July, and the adults emerge 2 weeks later.

Conservation status	**Least concern**

Monarch Butterfly
Danaus plexippus

Insects

Butterflies and moths

Butterflies

Factfile

Habitat	Temperate and tropical open habitats
Distribution	The Americas, Europe, Australia, Asia
Length	1.4 to 1.8 in
Wingspan	Up to 4.9 in
Female color	Orange and black
Male color	Same as female

Diet Monarch caterpillars eat poisonous milkweed leaves, while adults drink nectar from flowers, such as red clover, milkweed and thistle.

Fact Monarch butterflies are bright orange and black for a reason. The colors warn predators that this creature doesn't taste too good!

Conservation status	Least concern

Adonis Blue

Lysandra bellargus

Factfile

Habitat	Grassland
Distribution	Europe, Asia, Africa
Length	Up to .70 in
Wingspan	Up to 1.3 in
Female color	Brown and blue with orange crescents
Male color	Sky blue with a black line around the wings

Diet The larvae feed on leaves, leaving typical feeding damage of small pale disks. Adults feed primarily on a diet of nectar from marjoram and ragwort.

Fact This butterfly works together with ants. The ants protect the larvae, even burying them at night. The ants are attracted to the larval "honey glands."

Conservation status   **Vulnerable**

Red Admiral

Vanessa atalanta

Factfile

Habitat	Gardens, orchards, woodland
Distribution	Europe, North America, Asia
Length	.98 to 1.4 in
Wingspan	Up to 2.6 in
Female color	Dark with orange bands and white spots
Male color	Same as female

Diet Red admirals feed on tree sap, rotting fruit, bird droppings and the nectar of flowers such as the common milkweed, red clover, aster and alfalfa.

Fact Red admirals are known for their migratory behavior. They cannot survive in cold weather, so when winter sets in they fly to warmer climates.

Conservation status   **Least concern**

Small Copper Butterfly

Lycaena phlaeas

Factfile

Habitat	Savannah, grassland, mountains
Distribution	North America, Europe, Asia, Africa
Length	.40 to .79 in
Wingspan	Up to 1.2 in
Female color	Orange forewings with black spots
Male color	Same as female

Diet Small coppers eat nectar from flowers, including buttercups, clovers, butterfly weed, dwarf cinquefoil, wild strawberry, alfalfa and mountain mint.

Fact Male small coppers are among the most active of all butterflies. They regularly chase away other butterflies from their territory.

Conservation status   **Least concern**

Eastern Tiger Swallowtail

Papilio glaucus

Factfile

Habitat	Savannah, grassland, forest, mountains
Distribution	North America
Length	1.4 to 1.8 in
Wingspan	Up to 5.5 in
Female color	From yellow to bluish black
Male color	Yellow or yellow orange with black stripes

Diet The caterpillars of the eastern tiger swallowtail eat the leaves of woody plants. Adults drink the nectar of flowers from a variety of plants.

Fact These swallowtail tend to be solitary butterflies. Males search for a mate, flying from place to place actively looking for females.

Conservation status   **Least concern**

Scarce Swallowtail
Iphiclides podalirius

Factfile

Habitat	Woodland margins, open grassy areas
Distribution	Europe, Africa, Asia
Length	.87 to 1.0 in
Wingspan	Up to 3.5 in
Female color	Black and white stripes, with yellow tints
Male color	Same as female

Diet The larvae feed on foliage. Adults feed primarily on nectar. They often visit heathland as lavender flowers are one of their favorite foods.

Fact Scarce swallowtails are becoming rarer as their habitats are cleared. These butterflies are protected by law in some parts of Europe and Asia.

Conservation status   **Vulnerable**

Peppered Moth

Biston betularia

Insects

Butterflies and moths

Moths

Factfile

Habitat   Woodland, hedgerows, parks, gardens
Distribution   Asia, Europe, North America, Middle East
Length   .79 to 1.2 in
Wingspan   Up to 2.6 in
Female color   Mottled black and cream
Male color   Same as female

Diet   Most adult peppered moths feed on nectar from flowers, fruit pulps and leaves. Some of these moths have also been known to eat plant seeds.

Fact   Peppered moths are active at night. During the daytime they rest on the bark of trees, where they are camouflaged from predators such as birds.

Conservation status   **Least concern**

Garden Tiger Moth

Arctia caja

Factfile

Habitat	Gardens, farms, open areas
Distribution	Europe, Asia, North America
Length	.98 to 1.4 in
Wingspan	Up to 2.4 in
Female color	Black, brown, cream, orange, blue
Male color	Same as female

Diet The caterpillars feed on plants such as nettles, dandelions, brambles, docks, sunflowers and hollyhocks. Adults drink nectar from flowers.

Fact The caterpillars are so hairy that they have been given the nickname "woolly bears." The hairs cause irritation to protect the caterpillars from birds.

Conservation status   **Least concern**

Hummingbird Hawk-moth

Macroglossum stellatarum

Insects

Butterflies and moths

Moths

Factfile

Habitat	Gardens, meadows, forest edges
Distribution	Europe, Asia, Africa
Length	1.8 to 2.2 in
Wingspan	Up to 2.2 in
Female color	Grayish-brown forewings, orange hind wings
Male color	Same as female

Diet The adult moths feed on honeysuckle, lilac, snowberry and cranberry. The caterpillars eat honeysuckle, snowberry, hawthorns and plums.

Fact The hummingbird hawk-moth gets its name from the way that it hovers over flowers, sucking nectar from them, just like a hummingbird does.

Conservation status	**Not evaluated**

Cinnabar Moth
Tyria jacobaeae

Factfile

Habitat	Grassland, heathland, sand dunes
Distribution	Europe, Asia, North America, Australasia
Length	Up to .87 in
Wingspan	Up to 1.6 in
Female color	Black, red, gray
Male color	Same as female

Diet Cinnabar moth larvae eat the weed tansy ragwort. Tansy ragwort is toxic, and can be lethal to cattle and horses. Adults eat nectar from flowers.

Fact The caterpillars of cinnabar moths can become cannibals. When all available food has been consumed they will begin to eat each other.

Conservation status   **Least concern**

Giant Peacock Moth

Saturnia pyri

Factfile

Habitat	Mountain slopes, woodland, orchards
Distribution	Europe, Africa
Length	1.1 to 1.3 in
Wingspan	Up to 5.1 in
Female color	Mainly gray, white border and eyespots
Male color	Same as female

Diet The impressive caterpillars of the giant peacock moth feed on the foliage of a range of trees, including walnut, pear, ash and poplar.

Fact The giant peacock moth is the largest moth in Europe. The larvae are bright green in color and have a yellow stripe running along each side.

Conservation status	**Not evaluated**

Luna Moth
Actias luna

Factfile

Habitat	Woodland
Distribution	North America
Length	1.1 to 1.3 in
Wingspan	Up to 4.5 in
Female color	Yellowish green to pale bluish green
Male color	Same as female

Diet The caterpillars of the luna moth feed on foliage. The adult moth's only role in its short life is to reproduce and so it does not eat at all.

Fact The luna moth is nocturnal and is rarely seen in the daytime. It mimics leaves on the ground by remaining motionless to avoid predators.

Conservation status   **Not evaluated**

Buff-tailed Bumble Bee

Bombus terrestris

Insects

Bees, wasps and ants

Bees

Factfile

Habitat	Gardens, woodland, parks
Distribution	Europe
Length	.60 to .98 in
Wingspan	Up to 1.6 in
Female color	Yellow and black bands
Male color	Same as female

Diet The buff-tailed bumble bee is a herbivorous animal feeding primarily on nectar. It will eat pollen and honey if there is no nectar available.

Fact Unlike honeybees, bumblebees do not produce large amounts of honey. Their honey is stored just for feeding themselves and their young.

Conservation status — Near threatened

Honey Bee
Apis mellifera

Factfile

Habitat	Woodland, mountains, meadows, desert
Distribution	Africa, Asia, Europe, the Americas
Length	.31 to .47 in
Wingspan	Up to .98 in
Female color	Black and yellow
Male color	Same as female

Diet The honey bee feeds on nectar and pollen taken from flowers. They store food in honeycomb cells in their hive in order to see them through the winter.

Fact Honeybees live in large colonies. Each colony is made up of a queen bee, female workers and male drones. Drones do not have a stinger.

Conservation status   **Least concern**

113

Valley Carpenter Bee

Xylocopa varipuncta

Factfile

Habitat	Valleys, foothills
Distribution	North America
Length	.70 to .79 in
Wingspan	Up to 1.8 in
Female color	Black with a violet or bronze metallic sheen
Male color	Buff or golden colored

Diet The valley carpenter bee feeds on nectar from flowering plants. The female bee seems to show a preference for the wild passion vine.

Fact These bees nest in decaying wood, including unpainted man-made structures. They create tunnels in the wood to construct egg chambers.

Conservation status   Not evaluated

Common Wasp
Vespula vulgaris

Factfile

Habitat	Gardens, woodland, meadows
Distribution	Europe, Asia, North America, Australia
Length	.70 to .79 in
Wingspan	Up to 1.8 in
Female color	Black and yellow
Male color	Same as female

Diet The larvae of the common wasp feed on insects which the workers bring back to the nest. Adults eat high-energy sugary foods such as nectar and fruit.

Fact The main reason that wasps are feared by humans is their sting, which can be painful. The stinger can also be used more than once, unlike those of bees.

Conservation status   **Least concern**

European Wasp

Vespula germanica

Factfile

Habitat	Gardens, woodland, meadows
Distribution	Europe, Africa, Asia, America, Australia
Length	.47 to .60 in
Wingspan	Up to .79 in
Female color	Black and yellow
Male color	Same as female

Diet During the summer European wasps eat fruit and flower nectar. They will also collect honeydew and hunt for flies, mosquitoes and caterpillars.

Fact When a queen wasp creates a nest her first offspring are workers. They build their nest from "paper" made from saliva mixed with wood fibers.

Conservation status	**Least concern**

Cicada Killer Wasp

Sphecius speciosus

Factfile

Habitat	Well-drained soil
Distribution	North America, Europe
Length	1.5 to 1.7 in
Wingspan	Up to 2.9 in
Female color	Black and yellow stripes, brown wings
Male color	Same as female

Diet Adult cicada killer wasps feed on nectar from flowers, but their larvae feed on cicadas. Cicadas are paralyzed and slowly eaten by the larvae.

Fact Females sometimes work collectively to make a nest with multiple chambers. Each female stores her egg in an individual chamber.

Conservation status	**Not evaluated**

Paper Wasp
Polistes gallicus

Factfile

Habitat	Urban areas, forest, woodland, heath
Distribution	Worldwide (except Antarctica)
Length	.70 to .98 in
Wingspan	Up to 1.4 in
Female color	Yellow and black bands
Male color	Same as female

Diet Adult paper wasps feed only on the nectar from flowers. The larvae of paper wasps eat chewed up insects that the worker wasps hunt for them.

Fact After the queen wasp mates, she hibernates for the winter. In spring she will build a nest and begin raising worker wasps to help her build up her colony.

Conservation status   **Least concern**

118

Giant Wood Wasp

Urocerus gigas

Factfile

Habitat	Conifer forest
Distribution	Europe, Africa
Length	.60 to 1.6 in
Wingspan	Up to 2.0 in
Female color	Bright-yellow and black bands
Male color	Black thorax and orange abdomen

Diet The giant wood wasp lays eggs in timber. The larvae tunnel through the tree, eating the wood and fungi as they complete their development.

Fact The female has a long pointed tube which is often mistaken for a stinging organ, but in fact it is an ovipositor, which she uses to lay her eggs.

Conservation status	**Least concern**

Giant Ichneumon
Megarhyssa atrata

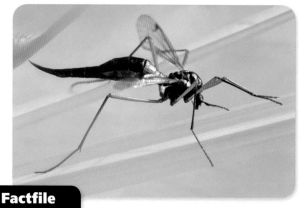

Factfile

Habitat	Forest
Distribution	North America
Length	1.4 to 1.5 in
Wingspan	Up to 2.4 in
Female color	Black body, yellow and black head, pale legs
Male color	Same as female

Diet Giant ichneumon are parasitic wasps. The female lays eggs on or near horntail wasp larvae and her young feed on the larvae. Adults are non-feeding.

Fact Females are at the highest risk of attack when laying eggs. During this process they have restricted movement so are vulnerable to predators.

Conservation status   Not evaluated

European Hornet

Vespa crabro

Factfile

Habitat	Woodland, farmland, forest, urban areas
Distribution	Africa, Asia, Europe, the Americas
Length	1.1 to 1.3 in
Wingspan	Up to 1.8 in
Female color	Brown and yellow
Male color	Same as female

Diet Hornets are a type of wasp. They will eat some tree sap but also eat animals. They hunt and eat flies, bees and many other types of insects.

Fact Hornets mix chewed plant fiber with saliva to form a paste. The paste is used to build nests. The nests are spherical, with an entrance at the bottom.

Conservation status   **Least concern**

Bald-faced Hornet

Dolichovespula maculata

Factfile

Habitat	Trees, bushes
Distribution	North America
Length	.47 to .55 in
Wingspan	Up to 1.3 in
Female color	Black and white with grayish wings
Male color	Same as female but with more white patches

Diet They feed on nectar, tree sap and fruit. They also prey on insects and other arthropods, chewing them up and feeding them to their larvae.

Fact Bald-faced hornets make nests by mixing chewed wood and saliva to make a paste. The paste dries into a paper-like material ideal for building.

Conservation status   **Least concern**

Black Garden Ant

Lasius niger

Factfile

Habitat	Gardens, scrubland, wetland, grassland
Distribution	Europe, Japan, North Africa
Length	.12 to .35 in
Wingspan	Wingless
Female color	Blackish brown
Male color	Same as female

Diet Black garden ants eat a wide range of food, including seeds, flower nectar, flies and other small insects, which they kill and take back to the nest.

Fact Small colonies can contain up to 5,500 individuals. Each colony is divided into groups: the queen ant, the female workers and the male workers.

Conservation status	**Least concern**

Leaf-cutter Ant
Atta cephalotes

Insects

Bees, wasps and ants

Ants

Factfile

Habitat	Forest
Distribution	Central America, South America
Length	.08 to .87 in
Wingspan	Wingless
Female color	Reddish brown
Male color	Same as female

Diet Leaf-cutter ants work together to collect leaf pieces and take them back to the colony. They create "fungus gardens" and eat the fungus that grows.

Fact Leaf-cutter ants live in huge underground nests that are connected by many tunnels. A single colony can contain up to 5 million members.

Conservation status	**Least concern**

Red Wood Ant
Formica rufa

Factfile

Habitat	Woodland
Distribution	Europe, Asia, North America
Length	.16 to .35 in
Wingspan	Up to .60 in (winged forms)
Female color	Dark-brown body, reddish thorax
Male color	Mainly black

Diet The red wood ant's primary diet is aphid honeydew, but it will also eat some insects and arachnids. They travel as far as 100 yards looking for food.

Fact Wood ants are found where there is plenty of dead wood for nest building. They are social insects living in colonies of up to half a million ants.

Conservation status	**Least concern**

Glossary

Abdomen The body region behind the thorax of an insect.

Algae Simple rootless plants that grow in sunlit waters.

Antennae Sensitive parts that project from the head. Sometimes called "feelers."

Aphids Tiny bugs that feed by sucking sap from plants.

Appendage A body part, such as an arm or a leg, connected to the main part of the body.

Aquatic Relating to water.

Arachnids The group of animals that includes spiders and scorpions.

Arthropod A group of animals that includes crabs, insects and centipedes.

Camouflage Colors or patterns that allow an animal to blend in with its background.

Cannibalistic Feeding on others of one's own kind.

Carnivorous To feed on the flesh of other animals.

Carrion The remains of dead animals.

Crustaceans Arthropods such as lobsters or crabs with jointed legs and two pairs of antennae.

Deciduous A tree or shrub that sheds its leaves annually.

Exoskeletons External skeletons that support and protect an animal's body.

Feces Waste matter discharged from the body.

Habitat The natural home of a species.

Herbivores Animals that feed on plants.

Hibernate To spend the winter in a sleeplike state.

Honeydew A sweet, sticky substance excreted by aphids.

Hydrate The process of maintaining a balance of fluids.

Infestations Invasions of animals in large numbers, typically causing damage or disease.

Insecticides A substance used for killing insects.

Invertebrates Animals without backbones.

Iridescent Producing a display of rainbowlike colors.

Latex A milky fluid found in many plants.

Mandibles A pair of appendages near the mouth of an insect used for grasping and cutting food, or for defense.

Mantids Slender predatory insects related to the cockroach.

Migratory Traveling from one area to another and back again each year.

Mildew A thick whitish coating of tiny fungal matter. Often seen growing on plants.

Nectar A sweet liquid that is produced by flowers.

Nocturnal Active at night.

Nutrients Compounds that provide plants and animals with nourishment.

Nymph A young larval stage of some insects.

Omnivore An animal that feeds on plant and animal matter.

Organic matter Material derived from organisms, especially decayed matter in soil.

Ovipositor The tube at the end of a female insect's abdomen, used for egg laying.

Parasitic An animal or plant living in or on another animal or plant in order to obtain nourishment.

Predators Animals that kill and eat other animals.

Prey An animal hunted by predators.

Psyllids Tiny plant-feeding insects.

Pupae/Pupate The stage between larva and adult in certain insects.

Savannah Hot grassland in Africa.

Scavenger An animal that feeds on decaying organic matter.

Secretions Substances, such as saliva or mucus, that are released from the body.

Sediment Matter that settles to the bottom of a liquid.

Siphon A tube used to convey liquid upward.

Solitary To exist alone.

Thorax The central body region of an insect between the head and the abdomen.

Toxic/Toxin A poisonous substance.

Index